Martin Trav

The Kids Are Alt Right

methuen | drama

LONDON • NEW YORK • OXFORD • NEW DELHI • SYDNEY

METHUEN DRAMA
Bloomsbury Publishing Plc
50 Bedford Square. London WC1B 3DP. UK
1385 Broadway, New York, NY 10018, USA

BLOOMSBURY, METHUEN DRAMA and the Methuen Drama logo
are trade marks of Bloomsbury Publishing Plc

First published in Great Britain 2019

Cover illustration by Ben Anslow
Series design by Louise Dugdale
Cover images: Skinhead (© Alamy / Danielle Casson),
Bandana (© Shutterstock / urfin), Skull (© Shutterstock / melazerg)

A catalogue record for this book is available from the British Library.

A catalog record for this book is available form the Library of Congress.

ISBN: PB: 978-1-3501-4052-3
ePDF: 978-1-3501-4054-7
ePub: 978-1-3501-4053-0

Series: Plays for Young People

Typeset by Country Setting, Kingdown, Kent CT14 8ES

To find out more about our authors and books visit www.bloomsbury.com
and sign up for our newsletters.

Martin Travers

Martin Travers' other plays include:

McLuckie's Line, co-written with, and starring, Martin Docherty, premiered at the Citizens Theatre in April 2018. The play toured nationally in September 2018 to critical acclaim and was seen by enthusiastic audiences across Scotland.

> '. . . stunningly vivid evocation of life on the front line in working class Glasgow . . . stories that have an energy and poetry that are funny, angry and elegiac'
>
> **** *The Scotsman*

> 'The lyrical, yet profane writing is a joy . . . feels like a spontaneous meeting with an old friend – the kind you love dearly' **** *The List*

Haw Hen, *Pigeon* and *Oor Carol's Christmas* for Glasgow-based In Cahootz. Directed by Kate Black, these three plays were written specifically for a large cast of community actors.

A Daurk Matier is a new full-length play in Scots about nineteenth-century working-class poets in Lanarkshire. Set against the backdrop of the Udston mining disaster; this play is part of Piston, Pen & Press: an Arts and Humanities Research Council funded project which aims to understand how industrial workers in Scotland and the North of England, from the 1840s to the 1910s, engaged with literary culture through writing, reading, and participation in wider cultural activities.

Martin conceived and scripted *Come Hell or High Water*. A new urban oratorio based on interviews with Scottish residents, asylum-seekers and refugees exploring what it is to be Scottish and British after the referendum to leave Europe. Directed by Guy Hollands with new songs and music by composer Finn Anderson, it premiered at the Citizens Theatre in March 2018 with a cast of twenty-five community actors and a live professional band. Extracts of the production were aired on Sky Arts in March and June 2019.

Supported by the National Lottery through Creative Scotland funding, Martin radically adapted Canadian writer and artist Heather Spears' novel *The Flourish* into a Scots stage play in 2017. Directed by Amanda Gaughan, there were three chamber performances of *Annville* (with live piano accompaniment created by Musical Director Karen MacIver) at the Citizens

Theatre, Scottish Storytelling Centre and the Institute of the Formation of Character in New Lanark.

Martin's short comedy *Life is Not a Rehearsal* was funded by the Noël Coward Foundation and performed by the Citizens Young Company at the Citizens Theatre as a curtain-raiser to Dominic Hill's production of *Hay Fever* in April 2017.

Martin's radical adaptation of Glasgow girl Jessie M. King's *The Little White Town of Never Weary* for Scottish Opera toured nationally in May 2016 and featured on the national news.

Martin's World War One musical *The Rifles* was performed in November 2015 by a cast of thirty, a nine-piece professional band, a piper and a choir of sixty students from New College Lanarkshire. Directed by Guy Hollands with music composed by Claire McKenzie, *The Rifles* was supported by a large-scale workshop programme and was seen by over 2,500 people.

His award-winning play *Scarfed for Life* has been performed numerous times by professional and non-professional companies and has toured Scottish prisons, schools and has been performed in theatre venues throughout the country. *Scarfed for Life* is currently studied in all Glasgow secondary schools.

His one-woman show *Miss Shamrock's World of Glamorous Flight* starring Pauline Knowles was part of the Play, Pie and a Pint autumn 2014 season at the Oran Mor.

Martin's musical adaptation of Theresa Breslin's multi-award-winning novel *Divided City* for the Citizens Theatre was the longest running participatory theatre in education project in the history of Scottish theatre, having been seen by over 20,000 people, with 2,500 young people from 110 schools having performed in a production.

In 2012 his play *Roman Bridge* was directed by Amanda Gaughan and was the centrepiece of the National Theatre of Scotland's Reveal season.

'eloquent and forceful'   **** *The Scotsman*

'a major new voice might just have been heard'
                                                            **** *The Herald*

'the greatest pleasure is Travers' muscular dialogue, at once flinty and naturalistic and richly lyrical, which marks him out as a new voice to relish in the future'   **** *The List*

The Kids Are Alt Right

This play was produced as a result of a partnership between the Scottish Government, Education Scotland, the Glasgow City Council programme 'Sense over Sectarianism' and the Citizens Theatre in Glasgow.

The drama was commissioned as an educational resource to provide a safe space to talk about a number of issues that young people face, including the effects of charismatic online influencers. This is part of the Scottish Government's wider efforts to build resilient critical thinkers who are equipped to challenge divisive narratives, and to safeguard vulnerable individuals who may be drawn into terrorism.

The research for the content of the play took place through consultation with young people in Glasgow Secondary Schools, South Lanarkshire Secondary Schools and Glasgow Clyde College's ESOL 16+ Programme. This method has been shown to be best practice in the production of previous similar materials.

This resource, *The Kids Are Alt Right*, is part of a wider package of teaching and learning resources which has been published on the Education Scotland National Improvement Hub website.

A lesson pack containing teaching notes, discussion points and linked educational activities has been produced to fully enhance the teaching capability and impact of the play. This lesson pack also contains relevant links to the experiences and outcomes from the Curriculum for Excellence.

Mark S. Adams
Social Inclusion Development Officer
Glasgow City Council

Thanks

A huge thanks to the teachers and students at Holyrood Secondary School, Whitehill Secondary School, Lanark Grammar School, St Andrew's and St Bride's High School and Clyde College for their help with the research for the story and who inspired some of the characters and language in the play.

And a special mention to Education Scotland, Mark Adams, the Scottish Government, Police Scotland, HOPE not Hate Charitable Trust, Shirley Mackie, Ruwayda Haroub, Mahad Abdullahi and Lyn Ma for their support and insight throughout the play's development.

Director and actors

The playwright would also like to thank director Guy Hollands and the following actors for their input into the development of the script: Qendresa Bajrami, Charlie Duncan, Luke Gallagher, Katie Garner, Jamie Leary, Shannon Lynch, Niamh McCarron, Lauren Mitchell, Alexandra Murray-Reynolds, Paula Nugent, Allan Othieno, Cameron Rickards, Tiia Stevenson and Cole Stewart.

The Kids Are Alt Right

dedicated to

Joseph the artist and Harry the poet

Characters
in order of appearance

Fatma
Bright seventeen-year-old girl born in Djibouti. She's a talented kick-boxer and physically very fit. She has lived in Scotland since she was an infant. Her stepmother is Scottish.

Miss Blaine
Politically active PE teacher at the school. She's close to Britney and Fatma and cares deeply about all the pupils' welfare.

Quinn
Seventeen years old. Jordan's pal. Wants to join the army. Addicted to his Xbox. Goalkeeper in school football team (when he goes to school). He lives with his mum, five younger brothers, his auntie, his cousin, his gran, three slobbery staffie dugs, a terrified cat and a parrot that swears. He would scoff deep-fried pizza for breakfast, lunch and dinner if he could afford it. Mostly – he eats toast.

Jordan
Britney's twin. He is fitba daft. Supports Barcelona. Captain of the school football team. Obsessed with his camera and taking photographs. He loves eating Britney's cereal to wind her up.

Maw
Britney and Jordan's harassed single mum. She works full time in a low-paid job for the council. Still dresses like she did as a teenager in the 1990s. Always singing Oasis songs.

Britney
Sixteen-year-old Scottish girl. She's really smart but pretends to be a bit of an airhead. Her long-term friendship with Fatma (since primary school) is under strain as she hangs out with a different group of shallow friends and is influenced by the Pretty Sisters. Is obsessed with her weight and how she looks. All she eats is cereal and red grapes.

Pretty Sisters
Very polite and upbeat. They model themselves on Kate Middleton. One has dark hair and one has fair hair. They dress ultra-feminine in expensive patterned blouses, immaculate and understated make-up and perfectly tonged and wonderfully conditioned hair. They act in unison – with one voice – mirroring each other's facial expressions and manners.

Mrs Quinn
Quinn's stressed-out mother.

Tartan Rebel
Scottish YouTuber. Pumped up ex-army alpha male. Wears a tartan baseball cap and tartan hoodie. He's charismatic and believable. Constantly tries to keep his hatred in check so that he seems reasonable and only wants true justice in Scottish society.

The Kids Are Alt Right *is the story of teenage friends torn apart by divisive right-wing influences. A fifty-minute ensemble play for a cast of six professional actors or a community or school cast of ten. In professional productions the actor playing* Jordan *will also play* Tartan Rebel. *The actors playing* Maw *and* Miss Blaine *will also play the* Pretty Sisters. Mrs Quinn *can be played by any cast member or could be a pre-recorded voice.*

Scene One

Fatma reads a section of an essay she's written.

Fatma   Things change. When you're young you think your pals will be your pals forever. That's not what happens. People change. Let you down. My dad says things are changing faster now. When he was a boy in his village in Djibouti he said the sky was always clear and calm and bright throughout the year. The stars were his YouTube. People were born there, they lived and laughed, and they died there of old age. Under an internet of silent stars. Governed by the seasons and the old ways. But then the angry men came with guns and knives and whipping sticks. People changed. Were forced to choose sides. Here in Scotland it's the same. No guns yet. But society and social media forces us to choose every day. To click or not to click that is the question. To like or dislike. Thumbs up – thumbs down. To choose in or out. Left or right. Cool or uncool. Black or white. Judge and jury. Us and them.

We hear the loud ringing of the school bell. **Fatma** *walks up a school corridor looking down at her phone.* **Miss Blaine** *hurries after and catches up with her.*

Miss Blaine   Fatma! Heard you got a prize! Read your essay on the school website. It's great. Not many girls are fantastic at PE *and* English. You're gonna be a star!

Fatma   I'd rather be a star-*fish* – hiding in the sand at the bottom of the sea. It's pure cringe, Miss Blaine. Wish I hadn't bothered. Britney went in a pure mad huff about it – says I was slagging off our friendship in it. I wasn't. Well . . . not really.

Miss Blaine   Fame has its pitfalls, Fatma. (*Trying to be cool but failing miserably.*) People can get *well jel'*. She'll be fine. It'll all blow over.

Fatma   Like a cloud of chlorine gas? Britney's changing. We've been besties since P 3. Now she's hanging out with the pink lip-gloss-slobbered, sparkly-clawed and contour-addicted divas. They are SO VACANT!

Miss Blaine   Now now. That's not nice. Okay, I'll admit some girls overdo the bronzing balls a tad when they go for the full Cleopatra but it's all about fitting in. It doesn't make them –

Fatma   Boring and nasty and superficial? Yeah, it does, you know. But that was just the start of it. Then my dad said the essay made him look like a dirt-poor nomad. A country pumpkin he said. I didn't want to point out he meant bumpkin. I was in enough manure. Then the Snapchat witches started. (*Witch voice.*) I hope your prize was a Stanley knife so you can use it to write your next essay on your black belly – (*her own accent*) that kind of loveliness. So remind me the next time I plan to pour my soul into print that I should drown myself in a bath of ice-cold mouldy bin juice first.

Miss Blaine   That's outrageous! Did someone actually say that to you?! If they did. I promise we'll read them the riot act. We're not having that kind of nastiness in this school. Did you screenshot it?

Fatma   I'm no snake, Miss Blaine. But even if I did screenshot it – they use fake accounts.

Miss Blaine   Fake or not – there must be a way to find out who's sending this bile.

Fatma   Adults are so naive. Snapchat-witching is the perfect crime. If you don't screenshot it – one stab then it's gone. No criminal. No weapon. No message. But the wound stays. In your head. I wouldn't worry, Miss Blaine. It's water off this black duck's back.

Miss Blaine   We can still –

Fatma   Rather you didn't.

Miss Blaine   I need to report this. We can't have –

Fatma   Report what? That the troublemaker daughter of
a refugee made up a story to get one of the polite *white* pupils
from the palaces up the golf course in trouble? You ask us to
be honest with you. So I'm honest. You need to be honest too.
There's no funny bunny-face filter that can fix this and make
it all right. Justice is a myth.

Miss Blaine   It's my duty. As a teacher in this school. It
sounds pure nanny state, I know, but we have a duty of care,
Fatma.

Fatma   Care? It would only make things worse! I don't need
that kind of attention in my life right now. Sorry – need to
run. Going to be late for my kick-boxing class.

Scene Two

Jordan *is trying to take arty photographs in an old abandoned factory.*
Quinn*, wearing a Union Jack skull snood around his neck, is smashing
up a wooden pallet and getting bored.*

Quinn   Whit A don't git is how ye hink rich fat-bergs ur
gonnae buy snaps ae this dump.

Jordan   It's an insight intae Scotland's wance glorious
industrial past int it? Gritty. Wet. Rusty. Cauld and bleak in a
mysterious soart ae wey. Rich Chinks and Yanks cannae git
enough Scottish rust.

Quinn   This place smells like a tramp's sh –

Jordan   Right, Quinn – like A says the last time. Ye kin hing
aboot wi me when A take ma pictures bit nae whingin'.

Quinn   Calm doon!

Jordan   You're the wan that needs tae calm it. That pallet's
took a right pounding. (*Putting on a head-teacher voice.*) Would you
say you had anger issues, Mister Quinn?

Quinn   Naw – A'd say A've gat freezin' ma bahookie aff issues. Waant tae start a fire?

Jordan   Naw! A don't waant tae start a fire! A waant tae take some pictures!

Quinn   Take some pictures ae the fire.

Jordan   An some pictures ae the polis when they're liftin' us?

Quinn   They'll never catch us.

Jordan   Nae fires!

Quinn *sulks and* **Jordan** *continues to take photographs.*

Quinn   Whit's his name?

Jordan   Who?

Quinn   That new refugee.

Jordan   In oor PSE class?

Quinn   Aye.

Jordan   Shar-suhin.

Quinn   See that? That winds me up. They come here. Wi name's that ur too haurd tae say. Cannae talk English.

Jordan   A widnae caw whit comes oot your geggie – or ever will come oot it – English.

Quinn   Ma Scottish English is mair English than his lingo.

Jordan   Aye – that widnae be hard bit. He's Somalian. He speaks Somali.

Quinn   Som-whit? That's no even a language. And anywey – he disnae speak *any* language. He disnae speak at aw! Nuhin' Three weeks. Husnae said snotters. Juist gies ye that look. That bomber look. That A'm gonnae cut your heid aff look. That A'm gonnae –

Jordan   Mebbe he' juist shy?

Quinn   Or hidin' suhin'.

Jordan Whit like? A bomb up his jouk?

Quinn You'll be laughin' oan the ither side ae yer face when the ither side's been blown aff. You watched that Tartan Rebel A wis tellin' ye aboot? He knows the score aboot these Jadies.

Jordan You mean jihadists?

Quinn How dae you always dae that? Pull me up aboot how A speak? It's pure annoyin'. A might be stupit bit A'm no daft.

Jordan You huv a bucket of donkey fungus for a brain and generally, you talk utter mush – that's why A feel the need tae point oot the odd grammatical error. Noo stoap feelin' sorry for yersel – make yersel useful. See whit's in that auld rucksack.

Quinn Nae chance, Jordan. Could be a tramp's Portaloo.

Jordan Or it could be stuffed wi cash. And some robber's stashed it in here when he's been pure parra. Could be worth thousands.

Quinn Hink sae?

Jordan (*bad Mexican accent*) Well, the silver stays in the hill until you dig it out, Gringo. (*His own accent.*) Know whit A'm sayin', hombre?

Quinn Naw – no really.

Jordan We won't know until ye look.

Quinn *pulls up his skull snood.*

Quinn This better no be honkin'.

He gingerly opens the rucksack and uses the torch on his phone to look inside.

Jordan Well?

Quinn *pulls out an old sleeping bag and throws it at* **Jordan***'s face.*

Jordan Ya durty bampot!

His muffled swearing is inaudible under the wet, clatty sleeping bag. He throws it away and shakes his hair and pats himself down like he's been attacked by beetles and rats.

Quinn   Class.

He shoves his hand into the rucksack and pulls out an ornate and lethal-looking zombie knife with a seven-inch blade.

Man! Whit a blade! Never foond anythin' like this afore. The only hing A've ever foond wis a wellie wi a frog in it. This is total treasure! How much dae ye hink it's worth?

Jordan   Three months and a fine?

Quinn   Ha ha. It's pure lucky we foond it.

Jordan   There's nothing lucky about a zombie knife, Quinny.

Quinn   Unlucky for some!

He stabs the rucksack with the knife.

Scene Three

Britney *and her* **Maw** *– drinking prosecco from a wine glass – are in* **Britney***'s bedroom. She recently had it totally redecorated. Out went the clutter and pop star posters and the teddy bears. It's now a pretty pink pastel box with a white bed, white curtains and white laminate flooring. And she's still raging that her mum wouldn't get her the expensive white carpet.*

Maw   When A wis your age A wis gittin' drunk three nights a week.

Britney *(sarcastically)*   Only the three? You've upped your game.

Maw   Smokin' fags. Blawin' smoke rings.

She purposely moves into **Britney***'s personal space.*

Maw (*singing to the tune of 'Cigarettes and Alcohol'*)   A wis lookin'
fur some act-sheeee-on bit aw A foond wis cigarettes an'
alcohol!

She mimes blowing smoke rings.

Britney   You really have got embarrassing me down to a fine
art. But you're wasting your time. You won't get a reaction.

Maw   That's 'cause yer eyebrows are so plastered oan ye
cannae move yer face.

Britney   My eyebrows are bloody perfect!

Maw   They're massive!

Britney   Like my dreams! They are a statement. My
eyebrows are me and I am my eyebrows. Perfect in every way.

Maw   Who waants tae be perfect? We were mental at your
age. Heavy pettin' in lavvies it pairties! Shoapliftin' lipsticks.
Flashin' bus drivers. Sticking chuggie intae the loaks ae
motors. Gittin' liftit. Gittin' aff wi fitba casuals. Pure tongues.

Britney   Pure tongues? Are you trying to make me yak?

Maw   Any reaction wid be helpful. A hud a happy healthy
teens.

Britney   You lived off fags and Twixes!

Maw   And Pot Noodles oan a piece fur breakfast! So whit?
At least A wis alive at your age!

Britney   I am *very* alive, Mother.

Maw   You're no very right in the heid, Britney. Sittin' oan
yer tablet in yer room fur oors oan end copying a skinny wee
gay man pitting oan make-up – juist tae waash it aff again?
You are worrying me sick. You're like a robot.

She mimes putting on lipstick – going round and round.

Britney   I'm happy being a robot. What's wrong with trying
to improve myself? *Crawl* out of my current circumstances.

Maw   Your circumstances ur better than mine ever wur. You don't know yer livin' ya wee –

Britney   I am going to get straight-A grades! Yes! I will excel! Escape to a prestigious university. Get a PhD. Marry a grotesquely successful businessman – who comes from a respected family. Going to have a *white* Mercedes-Benz people-carrier full of beautiful, talented and well-behaved *white* children with gloriously *white* teeth and live happily ever after in *white* shag-pile luxury. What's wrong with that?

Maw   You sound like a Tory.

Britney   Do you mean a Conservative?

Maw   You've chinged.

Britney   Improved.

Maw   Fur the worse. We ur working class, Britney. That's whit makes us good people. Salt of the earth. A people without history is like a tree without roots!

Britney   Jesus – here we go with the cheesy spliff-culture quotes – it's so nineteen-nineties. Where did you read that – on a packet of your large cigarette papers? You're such a drug addict!

Maw   You're such a robot! And A'll rip the Duracell batteries right oot ye if ye keep up your cheek.

Britney   Are you threatening me, Mother?

Maw   A'm no yer mother – A'M YER MAW!

Britney   You can choose your friends, but you can't choose your –

Maw   Don't go abandoning yer auld pals and family fir they posh androids you've been suckin' up tae. They're faker than their tans.

Britney   You're just jealous of my upgraded social circle.

Maw   They'll turn oan ye. You mark ma words. You better be going to the kick-boxing tonight.

Britney   I wanted to talk to you about that.

Maw   So talk.

Britney   I'm not going.

Maw   It's paid up. It's no cheap. So yer gaun!

Britney   It's not feminine. I'm not a tomboy any more.

Maw   It's pure empowerin'!

Britney   I'm not some weak lesbian feminist that needs empowering, Mother!

Maw   Not all feminists are gay, Britney.

Britney   But all lesbians are feminists, right? Fem-in-is-im. Even the word is a yack attack. It sounds like a leaking disease! It's so unappealing.

Maw   Ye widnae be sayin' that if were gittin' battered up an doon the hoose every night ae the week bi a drunk idiot.

Britney   That only happens in soap operas, Mother.

Maw   Godsake – you're the soap opera! Wid ye listen tae yersel? Should have called you Alexa! (*Robot voice.*) Does not compute – does not compute – does not –

Britney   Femininity has been drowning in degeneracy since – (*She mimes inverted commas.*) 'women's liberation' in the nineteen-sixties – thankfully we are starting to see the sagging fruits of feminist immorality rotting on the tree. Next thing you'll be demanding I play football!

Maw *yanks the tablet from* **Britney** *so she gets her full attention.*

Maw   A've spent a fortune oan aw that equipment ower the years. And the flights tae the championships are booked!

Britney   The championships are not for another nine months!

Maw   And that's why the flights tae Turkey were only forty quid each!

Britney   There's plenty of time to get a refund.

Maw (*frustrated but softening*)   I don't get it. You love kick-boxing. You're good at it, Britney. You and Fatma have a real chance of qualifying this time.

Britney   What if I don't want to qualify?

Maw   Won't waant tae whit? Don't you dare.

Britney   She's training to join ISIS. Just so you know.

Maw   Don't talk rubbish!

Britney   Read her blog!

Maw   Read my lips! (*She exaggerates mouthing the words.*) You. Are. Mental!

She walks out of **Britney**'s *room grabbing her make-up bag and closing the door behind her.*

Britney   Go filter your face.

Maw   A heard that! You're going to the kick-boxing the night!

Britney *sticks her tongue out at the door and clicks on a* **Pretty Sisters** *video on YouTube. She's mesmerised.*

Pretty One   Hi gang! As you know . . .

Pretty Two   We are . . .

Both   The Pretty Sisters!

Pretty One   Today we want to discuss the importance of good influencers.

Pretty Two   We underestimate the influence they have on us. Our world is full of influencers.

Pretty One   People who influence our lives.

Pretty Two   How we dress.

Pretty One   How we do our hair and makeup.

Pretty Two   And most importantly . . .

Pretty One   What we think.

Pretty Two   So, first off we will begin with defining what is an influencer?

Pretty One   It's a person you look up to.

Pretty Two   Most people are the product of the persons they surround themselves with.

Pretty One   When you are little it's our family.

Pretty Two   When we get older it's our friends.

Pretty One   If you have really good friends – upright, virtuous, noble friends then usually you will be like them.

Pretty Two   The kind of people you choose for your friends says everything about you.

Pretty One   And your state of mind.

Pretty Two   And what you actually wanna be.

Pretty One   And who you actually become.

Pretty Two   If you are influenced by someone who is pretty much empty intellectually or morally but might be physically beautiful . . . .

Pretty One   Then the only thing that you will strive for is outer beauty.

Pretty Two   That's such a huge trend nowadays.

Pretty One   People are just attracted to attraction.

Pretty Two   This is why you see so many people make celebrities their influencers.

Pretty One   These sort of celebrities – if you look at the messages they are promoting. It's things like drugs. Sex. A life of pure materialism.

Pretty Two   We shouldn't look up to shallow celebrities.

Pretty One   There are a lot of people in the right-wing movement – on YouTube – political commentators.

Pretty Two   They do videos on society or culture and I really admire them.

Pretty One   I really admire them too.

Pretty Two   Their different strengths.

Pretty One   In the American movement and European movement.

Pretty Two   There's so many people that I absolutely adore.

Pretty One   Very encouraging people that make the fight that we're currently going through seem a lot more hopeful and worthwhile.

Pretty Two   The right will win.

Pretty One   Just like they do in *Lord of the Rings*!

Pretty Two   Anyways – that's about it from this video.

Pretty One   We hope you got something out of it.

Pretty Two   Thanks so much for watching, guys.

Pretty One   We hope you enjoyed and we will see you soon.

Pretty Two   Bye-bye.

Pretty One   Bye-bye.

Pretty Two   And remember . . .

Both   It's all right to be white.

Scene Four

Quinn *is in his dark bedroom looking at his new zombie knife by the light from the screen of his phone. The room looks more like an adventure playground or underground militia bunker than a bedroom. There's camouflage netting (stolen from a fishing shop) pinned up all across the ceiling and draped down the walls. There are three sets of bunk beds forced in at daft angles in a room the size of a paddling pool. You can't see the floor for the stinking carpet of weeks-old crusty socks that cover it. There is a floor-to-ceiling pile of borrowed or shoplifted XBox games looking like Jack's beanstalk leaning against the top bunk.*

Mrs Quinn *screams into his room from outside.*

Mrs Quinn   Av hud enough ae the lot ae ye! How ma meant tae cope?! Wur no made ae money, sunshine! The sooner you're in the army the better! The next time you hink it's aw right tae hae *four* slice ae toast – you're haun'll be the fifth slice!

Quinn   Sorry, Maw – A wis hungry.

Mrs Quinn *(mimicking him)* 'Sorry Maw – A wis hungry'. Aye well – no as hungry as yer wee brothers ur noo thare's nae breid in the bloody hoose!

Quinn *pulls his headphones on to drown out his mum and watches a* **Tartan Rebel** *video on YouTube on his mobile.* **Tartan Rebel** *is filming himself live on his phone. He is lit by the neon lighting from the window from a takeaway food shop. He's breathing heavily – like he's about to share a terrible secret.*

Tartan Rebel   The Muslims wurnae a problem years ago by the way – 'at's 'cause Scotland didnae huv any Muslims! Honestly, troops – this boke-shoap is stinkin'. Don't know whit stinks ae BO the maiste – thaim or the cat-meat kebabs. When A say cat meat wur no talkin' Whiskas – A mean deid cats cooked up. A widnae lit ma dug eat whit these clat-bags punt. Always gi'en school lassies free chips. Ever noticed 'at? A huv. Us Scottish need tae defend oor lassies and wumen fae these predators. These clatty clowns huv nae respect fur women.

Knife attacks bi immigrant nut-joabs ur up. Did ye know that?
No feeling safe is noo normal. It's a problem aw ower the
country. Oor wumen – your daughters, your sisters, your
maws, your burds are terrified. Ivery wuman A know is scared.
You gaun tae ignore that? Dae ye know whit they caw it when
people pull thegither? Resistance. Patriotic resistance. Stabbings
and rapes?! You gaun tae dae nuthin aboot it? When in doubt –
the sword ae justice hus tae come out.

*He pulls his fist out of his hoodie pocket and holds it in front of the
screen – closer and closer until it blocks out the light.*

Scene Five

Fatma and **Britney** *are warming up at their kick-boxing training.
They are jogging on the spot, standing on the balls of their feet on thick
blue rubber mats. They play the entire scene on the balls of their feet.*

Fatma   My dad won't let me go on my own to Turkey.

Britney   Muslim girls go to Turkey all the time on their own.
That's how they sneak out the country to join ISIS. You'll be
fine. Just remember to get a return ticket.

Fatma   If this is your way of getting me to beg – you can
forget it.

Britney   Beg? Only dogs should beg. Are you saying I'm
asking you to act like a dog?

Fatma   I'm saying you're acting like a total idiot-child.

They go into rapid half-knee raises.

Britney   That's not a very nice thing to say.

Fatma   Well – if you weren't being so horrible, I might find
something nice to say to you.

Britney   I'm stopping kick-boxing. Big deal. Get over it.

Fatma   Is all this because of my essay?

Britney   Your *award-winning* essay? Oh no. It's much deeper than that.

They go into rapid full-knee raises.

We have different goals. Different cultures.

Fatma   You're the one that's being different.

Britney   Let's start with the obvious. I'm white – and you're not. I'm British – and you're not. I'm Christian – and you're not. I'm hot and you're not. I'm –

Fatma   A right pain in the glutes?! You and your stupid fads. Hours and hours tying strawberry-laces bracelets. If it's not red grapes – it's prawn cocktail crisps dipped in Irn Bru. Then it's green tea ice lollies – then it's watermelon lip gloss. But racist? Really? That's *so* pathetic.

They do basic jumping jacks.

Britney   Oh my God. You're the one that's pathetic. I state the blindingly obvious and you fly off the handle. Accusing me of racism?!

Fatma   Don't you dare try and turn this around and blame me!

Britney   Anger leads to defeat – remember? Stay in control.

They do criss-cross jumping jacks.

Fatma   Me stay in control? What about you? What about you staying in control of your senses! Those Pretty Sisters have got you brainwashed.

Britney   Me brainwashed? (*Sarcastically.*) L O L! Someone should read your blog – the police should read your blog – you sound like a religious fanatic. The West this – the West that. You can get arrested for that sort of hate speech.

Fatma   Hate speech?! I comment on world events. On how people are getting treated in Syria and Palestine. You don't have to read it. Free speech is a human right.

Britney   I couldn't agree more.

They bounce up and down in a front-facing side stance – switching sides periodically and varying their fight stances quickly.

Britney   And I don't think we should hang around together from now on. Like – at all.

Fatma   Suits me.

Britney   Good. I'm glad you're not taking it badly. Like I said. We are too different to be alike.

They slowly walk it out and take a few deep breaths.

Fatma   Not that I really care – but we've been dancing to Beyoncé videos together since we were eight years old. We used to keep a diary together. We've been all over the country to tournaments. Slept in the same bed. Since when did we get so different?

Britney   Honestly? Look in the mirror, Fatma. Look in your make-up bag. Look me in the eye and tell me you're from here.

Fatma   You're the one that should take a long hard look at yourself.

Britney   I have. And I like what I see.

Fatma   Do you know your problem?

Britney   I don't have any problems.

Fatma   Your problem is you're trying to fit in with girls who come from positions of privilege. In school and online. Because you don't come from that sort of background and you crave it. You crave it so much it's twisted you into an ugly racist GIF. But the tragic thing is – you never will come from that sort of background – and you never will fit in with them. You're their new fidget-spinner. Flavour of the month. Wee schemey Britney – the wee sook whose maw stinks ae weed and bleach and mops flairs for a livin. They'll chew you up and spit you out like cheap chewin' gum.

Britney *aims a kick at* **Fatma**'s *head. She blocks the kick and holds* **Britney**'s *foot in the air.*

Fatma   Speed, accuracy and power. That's all that's important. When you stretch too hard you'll end up with a ripped muscle. Is that sore? Muscle tears take months and months of healing. Is *that* sore? And that's only if you don't do anything to aggravate the healing process. Is *that* sore? Don't push yourself too far. Flexibility is a process gained over time – not overnight.

She pushes **Britney** *to the floor and walks away.*

Scene Six

Maw *is ironing in the kitchen. She's in her housecoat and flip-flops with wet hair and wearing no makeup.*

Maw (*singing to tune of 'Champagne Supernova'*)   Slowly walking down the hall faster than a cannonball. Where were you when we were *hingin'-claze-up-tae-dry*! Someday you will find me – caught beneath a landslide – in a Champagne Supernova in the sky.

Jordan *comes into the kitchen yawning uncontrollably and looking like a zombie that's been pulled through a hedge backwards.*

Jordan   A thought A heard seagulls. Bit when A gat doon the stair A realised it wis only you squawkin'.

He takes a box of cereal down from the shelf and pours two small glistening Alps of sugary orange flakes into a couple of bowls – finishing the box.

Maw   If we hud a cat and the cat dragged you intae the hoose – A'd huv tae git the cat put doon. Juist in case it had caught somehin' aff ye! Look at the state ae ye – yer like a vertical corpse.

Jordan   Seen yersel?

Maw   Cheeky wee . . . Whit time did ye git tae yer bed?

Jordan   FIFA time. Quinn beat me in the final. Cheatin'
wee −

Maw   You're gaun tae be late fur school!

Jordan   Naw A'm no. It's Saturday, Maw!

Maw   These bloody shifts. Honestly. A've no gat a clue if A'm
comin' or gaun. So − if it's Seturday, whit you daen oot yer pit
this early?

Jordan   Quinn's maw booted him oot this mornin'. He's
comin' roon.

Maw   Kicked oot? Whit's he done this time?

Jordan   No sure. Bit his maw's mental. Sometimes A hink
she juist dis it so she disnae need tae make his dinner for a
coupla days.

Maw   That ither bowl ae cereal better be hers!

She points up to the ceiling.

Jordan   Aye. Course it is.

Maw   A'm no waant you tae gie her any excuse tae throw
anither tantrum.

Jordan   Hink A'm in a fit state this mornin' for round two ae
World War Three? 'Sno oor fault Fatma battered her.

Maw   Battered my eye. A hink she's putting that sare leg
oan. Fatma widnae dae that. She's too professional.

Jordan   Mebbe she deserved it?

Maw   She keeps up this white supremacist routine much
langer an' she'll git whit's comin' tae her awright. She'll be
right-wing and homeless.

Jordan   A bit like Quinny then.

Maw   Yer wee pal's gat an excuse though − he's thick as
mince.

Quinn, *dragging a bin-bag half full of his clothes, comes to the kitchen door and knocks.*

Maw   Juist come in, Quinn son. Oor door's ayeweys open.

Quinn *comes in and wipes his feet.*

Maw   Ye hungry? Stick a coupla slice ae toast in, Jordan.

Quinn   A'm aff toast, Missus Devlin. Ma maw hit me ower the heid way the toaster this mornin'. Efter she read the letter. A've a lump the size ae a bylt egg oan ma heid.

Jordan   Whit letter?

Quinn   Fae the army. A didnae git in.

Jordan   A thought ye said ye'd done great in the first bit?

Quinn   Aye – hud tae run a mile and a hauf in nine minutes an forty-five seconds. A did it in eight minutes an ten seconds. Bit A failed the readin' an coontin' test dint A. Should hae been gaun in next month tae dae forty-two weeks ae trainin'.

Jordan   Don't worry, Quinny. You'll git another joab.

Quinn   It's aw right fur you, Jordan. You're brainy. You'll pass aw yer exams. The only thing A've ever passed is the parcel – playin' pass the parcel in primary. And even then A never won wance. Nae tub ae Celebrations fir me, ma man. (*His mood darkens.*) Thare's this hing. Pushin' me doon aw the time. Pushin'. Pushin'. A juist waant tae punch stuff.

Jordan   Somehin'll come up.

Quinn   Naw it won't.

Jordan   If ye think like that – then it won't.

Quinn   The only joab a could huv gat wis it the factory. An noo the factory's shut doon. There's nae joabs here, Jordan.

Maw   There is, Quinn. An A've done maiste ae thaim. Drappin' aff curries. Bar work. Waitressin'. Cleanin' jobs. Anything tae bring the money in. Ye used tae be able tae walk oot ae wan joab an straight intae another yin. Ye cannae dae that noo cause there's too many folk and no enough joabs. It's harder than it wis. A'm no sayin' it's no. Bit ye cannae gie up hope, son.

Quinn   Hope? A'm homeless! Ma maw says 'at's it. A'm oot the hoose. Whit dae A dae noo?

Jordan   She'll calm doon. Ye know whit she's like.

Quinn   Aye – A dae know whit she's like. She's a nightmare. Bit she widnae be a nightmare if the council wid gie us a proper hoose! She's been oan the list nine year. Then. Juist yisterday. See 'at empty five-apartment roon the corner fae us? The wan 'at used tae hae 'Yer maw's a mattress' spray paintit oan the back waw?

Jordan   That the wan wi the black burn marks aw the wey up the front fae a fire?

Quinn   Aye, bit no any mair. It's aw done up. Spankin' roof, the lot. Like a new hoose. An a hale lorry load ae Syrians juist moved in. Right tae the tap ae the list. Aw ma maw waants is a front and back door. How dae they git a front and back door?

Maw   That's a right bad corner, Quinn. A hoose like that wid only bring trouble tae yer door. Front *and* back.

Quinn   Cannae be any worse than it already is, Missus Devlin.

Maw   It's no the Syrians' fault they skipped the queue. They're probably juist relieved tae be alive. Whit's fur ye won't go by ye, son. Sit doon. Huv some cereal.

Scene Seven

In the changing rooms after P.E. **Britney** *is the last girl left. She's at the mirror on the wall and touching up her make-up.* **Fatma** *comes in and stands behind her. She's raging – livid.* **Britney** *sees her in the mirror but doesn't bother to turn round.*

Fatma   You missed a bit.

Britney   I'm not painting a fence.

Fatma   Looks like it from here.

Britney   Did you know Robertson's jam and marmalade was originally Scottish? Now it's owned by a multinational company. Quite sad really. The Pretty Sisters say globalisation is actually evil.

Fatma   I'm not here to talk about jam.

Britney   It used to have a golliwog on the front of it. Golly is American for dolly and, well, the second part – you can figure that out for yourself I'm sure. They stopped using the cute little black dolly with the big white eyes and beaming raspberry-red smile in two thousand and two. After lefty liberal pressure. It wasn't politically correct. Shame. Nobody's allowed to have a sense of humour any more.

Fatma *pulls a Stanley knife from her bag and accuses* **Britney** *with it.*

Fatma   Did you think this was funny too?

Britney *doesn't turn round.*

Britney   Is that a Stanley knife?

Fatma   You know it is. You sent it to my house!

Britney   Nope. Why would I? Why would I even bother?

She turns round casually and takes her phone out of her bag and checks her messages.

Fatma   I know it was you.

Britney   You could get into a lot of trouble bringing that into school. Bet it doesn't even have a blade in it.

Fatma   You know it does!

She flicks the Stanley knife open and holds it up so **Britney** *can see that it does.*

Britney   Say cheese!

She takes a photograph of **Fatma** *angry and holding the open Stanley knife.*

Fatma   Delete that.

Britney   Now the whole world will know you're a psycho.

Fatma   Why you doing this?!

Britney   Me doing this?! You're doing this! I never sent it. It's not my style.

Fatma   Don't believe you.

Britney   Don't actually care. I've a good idea who did. You're right – they're so childish. But it is quite funny.

Miss Blaine *comes in carrying a net full of netballs. They don't see her.*

Fatma   Give me the phone!

Britney *turns her phone round so that* **Fatma** *can see the photograph.*

Britney   You can definitely tell this was taken in school. Bang goes the sports scholarship!

Fatma *lunges at* **Britney** *to get the phone.* **Britney** *holds the phone above her head and hits a button and posts the photograph on Snapchat.*

Britney   Ping!

Miss Blaine (*shouts*)   RIGHT GIRLS – THAT'S ENOUGH!

As **Fatma** *grabs for the phone she drops the open Stanley knife. As it falls it scratches* **Britney**'*s leg.* **Britney**'*s phone flies out of her hand and lands hard – cracking the screen. During the rest of the scene both* **Britney** *and* **Fatma**'*s phones ping repeatedly as people comment on the picture* **Britney** *has just posted.*

Britney   Stupid bitch! You cut me!

Fatma   And you just ruined my life!

Miss Blaine *runs over to them.*

Miss Blaine   Fatma! Sit there. Britney – let me see your leg.

Fatma *sits down on a bench.* **Britney** *holds her leg out so* **Miss Blaine** *can see it.*

Britney   She stabbed me.

Miss Blaine *examines* **Britney**'s *leg.*

Miss Blaine   Now there's no need to be so melodramatic. It's a bad scratch. You'll be fine.

Britney   A scratch is a cut – she stabbed me!

Fatma   I never meant to stab you.

Miss Blaine   It's a scratch – you never *stabbed* anybody.

Britney *picks up her phone and sees the screen is broken.*

Britney   And she's broke my phone! Do you know how much it costs to get a screen fixed?! Want her charged!

Miss Blaine   Enough, Britney! It's only a phone – for Christ's sake. (*To* **Fatma**.) What happened?

Britney   She attacked me – Want her done.

Miss Blaine   I saw what happened. She didn't attack you. Now – be quiet! (*To* **Fatma**.) Well?

Fatma   I was sent that through the post.

Miss Blaine   Oh my God – that's sick. Why didn't you call the police?

Fatma   I'm from Djibouti. We don't trust the police.

Britney   They don't trust you either!

Miss Blaine   You can't bring a bladed implement into school, Fatma!

Britney   She threatened me with it.

Fatma   I thought she sent it to me. Wanted to confront her with it. Wasn't thinking straight.

Britney   Wasn't me. Not my style.

Fatma   Then she took a photograph of me holding it – and now she's posted it online. I was just trying to stop her. And I dropped the knife.

Britney   She attacked me. That's a weapon. Want her done.

Miss Blaine   Nobody's getting *done*, Britney!

She picks up the Stanley knife.

Did you send this to her?

Britney *laughs in disbelief. She can't believe she's the one being questioned.*

Miss Blaine   This bullying has to stop.

Britney   Couldn't agree more. Want her expelled. I'm not safe at school with her being here.

Miss Blaine   Fatma is the one getting bullied, Britney. Stop being such a wee . . .

She stops herself saying something she shouldn't.

This ends here! Now. Britney – get to your next class.

She sits down beside **Fatma** *– putting her arm around her.* **Britney** *grabs her things – taking a photograph of* **Miss Blaine** *and* **Fatma** *as she leaves.*

Britney   You're DTM, Fatma. Psycho!

Miss Blaine   Enough, Britney. I'll speak to you later. Get out!

As **Britney** *storms off* **Fatma** *starts crying. She's devastated.*

Fatma   Britney didn't send it, Miss Blaine. Snapchat witches. *They* sent it. *They* sent it. *They* sent it.

Scene Eight

Quinn *is sitting in a park on his phone, waiting on* **Jordan** *coming out of school. He is eating a deep-fried pizza from the chip shop and watching* **Tartan Rebel** *as he streams a post live.* **Tartan Rebel** *is filming himself outside a court. He is surrounded by well-wishers and hangers-on – most of them have their faces covered by skull snoods and scarves. He's pumped up with a sense of victory and relief.*

Tartan Rebel   As maist ae ye know. A wis arrestit a coupla days ago. In ma ain hame. It night. Dragged oot ma hoose. Handcuffed. Accused ae a hate crime. A hate crime?! A stood ootside a shoap-ful ae – need tae watch whit A say here. Stood ootside a clatty shoap an aw A said wis – we huv tae defend oorsels. Fae criminals. Defend oor wummen an young lassies fae rapists. Said it's oor patriotic duty. An some snake complained tae the polis. Said A wis incitin' racial hatred. Is 'at a sick joke or whit? 'At's the court ahint us. The charge hus been chucked oot!

The well-wishers and hangers-on all cheer.

Alexander the Great said 'A'm no scared ae an army ae lions led bi a sheep; A'm scared ae an army ae sheep led bi a loin.' We're the new lions. The new kings. Nae mair suppression ae free speech. Nae mair lies. Nae mair polis intimidation!

Quinn *sends the* **Tartan Rebel** *a message. The* **Tartan Rebel** *reads it.*

Tartan Rebel   'At's a message fae wee Quinny juist in. Last week he donated his last tenner tae help piy fir ma lawyer. Thanks, wee man. You're wan ae the good guys. Muslims gat a brand-new council hoose roon the corner fae his maw's. Juist like 'at. Nae waitin'. Nae nine years oan a hoosin list fir they beggars. We gaun tae sit back an lit this disease keep spreadin'? Naw – no chance! No any mair. The morra. Seven a-cloak. Everybody watchin' this. The real men oot thare watchin' this. We're aw gaun tae this hoose. An we're aw gaun tae protest until they git the message. Contact Quinny direct fur the details. An don't worry, wee man. A'll be thare tae! A've been hinkin a lot aboot this when A wis in custody. It's past the point ae nae return. Past the point ae turnin' a blind eye. Turnin' the ither cheek. When yer fed up bangin' yer heid aff a brick waw. Whit dae ye dae? Ye take a sledge hammer tae the waw!

Quinn's *phone starts to ping over and over and over again with messages. He feels like he's going to spew up.*

Scene Nine

We hear a school bell ringing. **Britney** *is waiting for* **Miss Blaine** *in a corridor.* **Miss Blaine** *sees* **Britney** *and thinks about turning back before taking a deep breath and going over to confront her.*

Britney   Did you report her?

Miss Blaine   You know there was nothing to report.

Britney   Read her blog. She's an extremist. That's the second time she's attacked me. She did it at kick-boxing. (*She points to her calf muscle.*) See that bruise there? That was her. And she's attacked me again today. I'm glad you came in when you did. Who knows what she would have done if you hadn't.

Miss Blaine   Britney – Fatma told me everything.

Britney   She could have cut my throat.

Miss Blaine   Why are you being so awful to her? Why are your friends being so awful to her? Is it just because she's black? Muslim?

Britney   They're not my friends any more, Miss Blaine. Sending a knife through the post? That's what cowards do. I'm not a coward. And I won't be hanging round with cowards from now on. And I think I'll change my look. Be a bit more individual. I'm going to be a lone wolf.

Miss Blaine   If you keep talking like that I'll need to inform the head teacher. We have a duty of care at this school. You might need to speak to someone.

Britney   Yes. I do. I really do. I need to speak to someone who can help me. Listen to me. So I'm going to speak to the police. Actually, I'm going to speak to them right now. And I'm going to tell them about this afternoon. That you didn't do anything. That you saw everything and you didn't do anything other than cover up her crime. Here. Look.

She turns the smashed screen of her phone around to let **Miss Blaine** *see the photograph she took of her and* **Fatma**.

Britney   Look. See? You have the Stanley knife in your hand. The screen's smashed but I'm sure you can still see it. Do you know how embarrassed I'm going to be for months? My mother can't afford to replace a smashed screen. She can hardly afford to buy cereal these days. A phone like this? It's like coming to school every day for months wearing ripped tights. Do you have any idea what that's going to feel like?

Miss Blaine   Wait, Britney. If it means that much to you. I can pay for a new screen.

Britney   That would be great. But it's not going to stop me doing this.

She phones the police.

Hello? Yes. I'd like to report a crime. I was attacked at school today. Britney Devlin. D-E-V-L-I-N. Sixteen. One hundred and twenty-six Strathmuir Place.

Scene Ten

Jordan *is playing keepy-uppy with an old football outside the local police station. He has a pizza box in his hands.* **Quinn** *comes out looking tired and lonely.*

Jordan   Quinn!

Quinn   How did you know A –

Jordan   Yer maw phoned us. A said A'd come doon and git ye. She said you've been charged wi possessin a knife? Wis it that stupit zombie knife?!

Quinn   Aye.

Jordan   A knew you shouldnae hae kept that. Whit ye daen cairyin a knife aboot wi ye onyweys?!

Quinn   Tae defend masel!

Jordan   Fae whit?! Orcs?! Fire-breathin' dragons?! Bet the polis didnae buy that.

Quinn   A juist telt them A foond it. They didnae believe us.

Jordan   You've no exactly gat an honest face, Quinn. Did ye say A wis thare when ye foond it? A'll back ye up.

Quinn   Didnae waant tae git ye intae trouble an aw. Breken intae abandont factories is probably against the law.

Jordan   Never thought ae that. Yer right – probably is. So whit happened?

Quinn (*sighing deeply*)   It's a lang story.

Jordan   An it'll bi even langer if ye don't juist come oot wi it.

Quinn   Mynd 'at faimily 'at gat the hoose roon the corner? They Syrians.

Jordan   Aye. An A don't like where this is gaun.

Quinn   A telt the Tartan Rebel aboot it. Then he telt thoosands a folk aboot it. Said A'd tae organise a protest outside their hoose last night. Kept gittin' aw these messages fae bampots – pure heid-cases sayin' they were comin' an *we* wur gaun tae burn the hoose doon. Didnae know whit tae dae. Didnae waant thaim dyin' in a fire. Weans an aw that. So A went roon early. Quarter tae seven. Wis gaun tae try an make sure naebidy gat burnt. Waitit. An waitit. A hud ma snood up – it wis freezin'. Naebidy came.

Jordan   The world is fulla keyboard arsonists, ma man.

Quinn   Nut. Ye'v loast us.

Jordan   What A'm sayin' is. If ivery nugget 'at threatent tae start a fire online actually startit a fire – the world wad hae burnt doon a lang time ago.

Quinn (*still doesn't understand*)   Bit naebody showed up – 'at's whit A'm sayin'. Nae fires.

Jordan (*winding him up*)   Nae fire brigade then?

Quinn   Naw. Nae fire – nae fire brigade.

Jordan   So then whit?

Quinn   Hauf-eight an A'm like – A'm getting tae. Bit wan ae they Syrians must hae phont the polis.

Jordan   Nae wunner.

Quinn   Two cops arrived. Searched and liftit. Charged.

Jordan   Did ye tell thaim aboot the Tartan Rebel?

Quinn   Course A niver! Said A wis lookin' fur ma hoose key. That A'd drapt it.

Jordan *hands* **Quinn** *the pizza.*

Jordan   Here. Probably cauld.

Quinn   Prefer it cauld.

He opens the box and starts to devour it.

Whit they wee black bits?

Jordan   Olives.

Quinn   And the wee rid bits?

Jordan   Peppers.

Quinn   It's magic!

Jordan   'At's cause it's no been deep-fried, ma man. Ye need tae broaden yer horizons, Quinny. Aboot pizza – *and* people. See the new dude in the class. The refugee?

Quinn   Aye.

Jordan   He's some fitba player. World class. Wi him in the
team we might even win the cup this year. An see if you hink
your life's juist went doon the lavvy? Wait till ye hear his story.
Somalia's nuts. He wis held hostage bi people-traffickers. In
Libya. Burnt aw doon his back and backside wi burnin hoat
plastic. Dripped it aw ower his skin – oan fire! Tied his haunds
up wi cables very night. Demandit money fae his maw. Ten
thousand dollars. When she couldnae piy it they gave him a
total tankin'. Burst his ankles open wi a rifle. A bloody rifle?!
When the people-traffickers were busy fixing a tyre oan the van,
he pit oan four pairs ae soacks tae stop the blood drippin' aw
ower the place an done a runner. Then it took him a ful year
tae git fae Libya tae here. A year! An ye wunner how he's shy?

Quinn   'At's mental.

Jordan   And true. Mon – let's git you up the road. Yer maw
waants tae see ye.

Scene Eleven

Britney *is in her bedroom, studying – she's reading a large hard-backed
book on World War Two.* **Maw** *storms in. She's seething with rage.*

Maw   A'm juist aff the phone tae Fatma's faither. A've niver
been so mortified in ma life! When war ye gaun tae tell me
whit happen?

Britney   I knew you'd react like this.

Maw   React like this?! Like this?! This is nothin!

She rips the textbook from **Britney***'s hands.*

Maw   Whit rubbish you readin noo? Hilter?! Bloody Hitler?!
No in ma hoose yer no.

She throws the history book against the wall.

Britney   It's research – for a history essay. That's from the school library.

Maw   A don't care!

Britney   You should. You'll need to pay the fine if it's damaged. Did you know that before the war the German government set up a scheme called Strength Through Joy? It gave workers rewards for their work – theatre trips, evening classes, picnics, and even free holidays. I'm sure you would love a free holiday. I know I would.

Maw   Whit happened?!

Britney   It's none of your business. But I'm sure the police will give you a copy of my statement if you ask. You are my mother after all.

Maw   Fatma's been suspended. Indefinitely suspended. She's getting charged! Miss Blaine's been reported to the General Teaching Council. She could lose her right to teach!

Britney   Miss Blaine took sides. That's unforgivable. Horribly unprofessional. And Fatma's such a selfish beanbag. All she's worried about is getting to get to the kick-boxing championships. She tried to set me up. To get me back for moving on with my life. She's always been such a leech. A dangerous attention-seeking leech. Maybe she can write her next *award-winning* essay from solitary confinement.

Maw   This isnae funny! Ye didnae need tae phone the polis!

Britney   I did actually. There's nothing funny about it. I was attacked.

Britney's **Maw** *grabs her and throws her on to the bed.*

Maw   Attacked my backside! You've juist wrecked two good people's lives. Two people who cared aboot ye! This *phase* – this effen attitude. This cruelty! It stoaps right here. Wake up, hen!

Britney   I'm very awake, Mother. More awake than I've ever been.

Maw   A don't know you any mair!

Britney   You never did.

Maw   You're nae daughter ae mine!

She slams the door on **Britney** *as she storms out of the room.*

Britney (*shouts*)   That's a relief!

She picks up her tablet and make-up bag and sits down on her bed. She uses a cotton pad to wipe off the heavy make-up she's wearing – all the make-up will be removed by the end of the scene. She types 'Pretty Sisters' into YouTube, puts on her headphones and clicks 'play'.

Pretty One   Hi gang! As you know . . .

Pretty Two   We are . . .

Both   The Pretty Sisters!

Pretty One   So much bad press has been on social media recently about the so-called continued rise of violent and monstrous right-wing extremism. We felt you might need a little bit of TLC.

They both blow kisses at the camera and laugh.

Pretty Two   We're not violent.

Pretty One   Or monstrous . . .

Both   . . . but we are right-wing!

Pretty Two   You have to ignore all that negativity.

Pretty One   Keep making change in your community and personal life.

Pretty Two   Don't let them connect you or what you believe in with shootings or explosions.

Pretty One   That's them trying to smear you.

Pretty Two   But you can't walk away either – right?

Pretty One   Yeah, definitely. Don't let them force you to abandon your country.

Pretty Two   Keep trying to fix your country.

Pretty One   Migrants don't try to fix their countries. They discard them.

Pretty Two   And who knows what terrible crimes they are running away from too, you know?

Pretty One   I'd say so, yeah.

Pretty Two   These weak opportunists abandon their countries. Leaving a trail of burned-out cars and buildings behind them.

Pretty One   And most of them leave their wives and children behind. Right? Let's not forget that.

Pretty Two   They abandon their responsibilities as fathers and husbands. And as citizens.

Pretty One   So that links us neatly into what we want to talk about now.

Pretty Two   Today's main topic is going to be . . .

Both   Abandonment.

Pretty One   Abandonment is feeling let down and insecure.

Pretty Two   Normally by the people around you. And also governments.

Pretty One   Living with abandonment experiences creates toxic shame and fear in us.

Pretty Two   It stops us from being the best we can be.

Pretty One   The shame arises from the painful message implied in abandonment: 'You are not important.'

Pretty Two   'You are not of value.'

Pretty One   This is the pain from which people need to heal.

Pretty Two   But you got to fight to get better. To survive sometimes you need to fight until your knuckles are bleeding. We bleed to heal, right?

Pretty One   So when people close to you attack your view points and beliefs? That backlash and opposition? That's toxic abandonment.

Pretty Two   And toxic abandonment really sucks!

Pretty One   There's the easy way – and there's the right thing to do. You have to follow your moral compass.

Pretty Two   Even if it means distancing yourself from people around you who are abandoning you.

Pretty One   Even your family.

Pretty Two   Yeah. Totally. When we started doing this? Defending the right? We got abandoned.

Pretty One   But we kept speaking up.

Pretty Two   We did that because we are passionate about the future of the world.

Pretty One   We all hit crossroads. It's easy to turn back. Turn back to who and what you already know.

Pretty Two   But to go on. Into the future. That's the right thing to do.

Pretty One   It would be cowardly not to.

Pretty Two   We know you are all looking for a way to change things. A way to contribute.

Pretty One   Who wants to feel desperately hopeless, right?

Pretty Two   In a world filled with lies you have a real opportunity here to make some change.

Pretty One   That's why we need you in the movement.

Pretty Two   Our identity comes from our community.

Pretty One   This is our generation's time to shine.

Pretty Two   The future belongs to us.

Pretty One   Your voices are so needed.

Pretty Two   Italian voices. Austrian voices. Spanish voices. French voices. Canadian voices. English voices.

Pretty One   And don't forget Scottish voices too, right?! Our Brave Hearts in the north are *sooo* important. If you want to connect in Scotland. Check out Tartan Rebel's YouTube channel. He's so well respected in our community.

Pretty Two   He's awesome. Let's collab with him on something soon.

Pretty One   That's an awesome idea. I love his hat!

Pretty Two   Me too! Look out for our new updates on defending Europe soon.

Pretty One   So that's about it for now. That's what we wanted to say on the topic of abandonment.

Pretty Two   And to clarify why we do what we do and why we got into it.

Pretty One   We hope you got something out of it.

Pretty Two   Thanks so much for watching, guys.

Pretty One   We hope you enjoyed and we will see you soon.

Pretty Two   Bye-bye.

Pretty One   Bye-bye.

Pretty Two   And remember . . .

Pretty One   Don't let them into your head.

Pretty Two   Don't let them de-platform your convictions.

Both   It's all right to be alt right!

Britney *puts down the cotton pad she's using to take off her make-up and types 'Tartan Rebel' into YouTube.*

The End.

Glossary

'At   That
'Sno   It's not
A   I
A'd   I would
A've   I have
Abandont   Abandoned
Aboot   About
Act-sheeee-on   Action
Ae   Of
Aff   Off
Ahint   Behind
An aw   As well
Anither   Another
Arrestit   Arrested
Arsonists   People who wilfully and maliciously set fire to property
Awright   Alright
Ayeweys   Always
BO   Body odour
Bahookie   Bum
Bampot   Bad or unhinged person
Bampots   Crazy people
Battered   Attacked
Bi   By
Bit   But
Blawin'   Blowing
Boke-shoap   Derogatory term for an eating place that isn't clean
Breid   Bread
Breken   Breaking
Burds   Derogatory term for girlfriends
Bylt   Boiled

Cairyin   Carrying
Cannae   Can't
Cauld   Cold
Caw   Call
Celebrations   Brand of mixed chocolates
'Champagne Supernova'   A song by Oasis
Chinged   Changed
Chinks   Derogatory term for Chinese people
Chuggie   Chewing gum
Clat-bags   Unclean people
Clatty   Unpleasant, dirty
Coontin   Counting
Coupla   Couple of
DTM   Dead to me
Daen   Doing
Deid   Dead
Didnae buy   Did not believe
Didnae   Did not
Dint   Didn't
Djibouti   Republic of Djibouti, a small country located in the Horn of Africa. It is bordered by Eritrea, Ethiopia and Somalia
Done   Charged with a criminal offence
Done up   Redecorated
Doon   Down
Drappin   Dropping
Drapt   Dropped
Durty   Dirty
Fae   From
Fags   Cigarettes
Faimily   Family

Fatberg   Congealed mass of non-biodegradable matter in a sewage system

FIFA   Soccer video game

Fitba casuals   Football casuals: gangs of young men in the 1980s and 1990s in Britain known for attending football matches, fighting and hooliganism, and wearing expensive designer clothing

Flairs   Floors

Foond   Found

Ful   Full

Fulla   Full of

Fur   For

Gat   Got

Gaun   Going

Geggie   Mouth

Gie   Give

Gien   Giving

Gies   Gives

GIF   A series of images or soundless video that loop continuously

Git   Get

Gittin'   Getting

Godsake   For God's sake

Gonnae   Going to

Gringo   A person, especially an American, who is not Hispanic

Hale   Whole

Hame   Home

Hauf   Half

Haun'll   Hand will

Haurd   Hard

Heid   Head

Heid-cases   See Bampots

Hing   Hang/Thing

Hink   Think

Hombre   Man

Honkin'   Very smelly

Hoose   House

Hoosin   Housing

Hud   Had

Husnae   Hasn't

Huv   Have

Int   Isn't

Irn Bru   A brand of carbonated soft drink

ISIS   Islamic State in Iraq and Syria

It   At

Ither   Other

Ivery   Every

Joab   Job

Jouk   Jumper

Juist   Just

Keepy-uppy   A ball game where the player tries to keep the ball in the air as long as possible

Kin   Can

Lang   Long

Langer   Longer

Lassies   Girls

Lavvies   Lavatories

Lavvy   Lavatory

Liftit   Arrested

Lingo   Language

Loaks   Locks

Loast   Lost

Ma   My

Mair   More

Maiste   Most
Masel   Myself
Maw   Mother
Mebbe   Maybe
Mental   Crazy
Mortified   Acutely
  embarrassed
Motors   Cars
Mynd   Do you remember
Nae   No
Naebidy   Nobody
Naw   No
Niver   Never
No   Not
Nut   No
Nuthin   Nothing
Nut-joabs   Crazy people
Oan   On
Oasis   An iconic English rock
  band formed in
  Manchester in 1991
Onyweys   Anyway
Oors   Hours
Oorsels   Ourselves
Oot   Out
Ower   Over
PE   Physical Education
class
PhD   Doctor of Philosophy
PSE   Personal and Social
  Education
Paintit   Painted
Pairties   Parties
Parra   Paranoid
Phont   Telephoned
Piece   Sandwich
Pit   Bed
Portaloo   Chemical toilet

Pot Noodles   A brand of
  instant noodles
Quid   A British pound
Roon   Around
Sae   So
Sare   Sore
Schemey   Someone who lives
  in a housing scheme
Seturday   Saturday
Shoapliftin'   Shoplifting
Shouldnae   Should not
Snood   A tubular scarf
Snotters   Nasal mucus
Soacks   Socks
Soart   Sort
Staffie dug   Staffordshire bull
  terrier
Stanley knife   A brand of
  heavy-duty utility knife
Startit   Started
Stoap   Stop
Strawberry laces   Strawberry
  flavour sweets
Stupit   Stupid
Suhin'   Something
Tae   To
Tankin'   See Batter
Tap   Top
Telt   Told
Thaim   Them
Thegither   Together
Thoosands   Thousands
Threatent   Threatened
Twix   A brand of chocolate
  biscuit bars
Ur   Are
Us   Me
Waant   Want

Waants   Wants

Waw   Wall

Wee   Small

Weed   Marijuana

Well jel'   Very jealous

Wey   Way

Whingin'   Whinging

Whiskas   Brand of cat food

Whit   What

Wi   With

Wid   Would

Widnae   Wouldn't

Wis   Was

Wumen   Women

Wunner   Wonder

Wur   Were

Wurnae   Were not

Yak   Sick

Yanks   Diminutive term for American people

Ye'v   You have

Yer   Your

Yersel   Yourself

Zombie knife   An ornate and deadly-looking knife banned in Britain

Methuen Drama Modern Plays

include work by

Bola Agbaje
Edward Albee
Davey Anderson
Jean Anouilh
John Arden
Peter Barnes
Sebastian Barry
Alistair Beaton
Brendan Behan
Edward Bond
William Boyd
Bertolt Brecht
Howard Brenton
Amelia Bullmore
Anthony Burgess
Leo Butler
Jim Cartwright
Lolita Chakrabarti
Caryl Churchill
Lucinda Coxon
Curious Directive
Nick Darke
Shelagh Delaney
Ishy Din
Claire Dowie
David Edgar
David Eldridge
Dario Fo
Michael Frayn
John Godber
Paul Godfrey
James Graham
David Greig
John Guare
Mark Haddon
Peter Handke
David Harrower
Jonathan Harvey
Iain Heggie

Robert Holman
Caroline Horton
Terry Johnson
Sarah Kane
Barrie Keeffe
Doug Lucie
Anders Lustgarten
David Mamet
Patrick Marber
Martin McDonagh
Arthur Miller
D. C. Moore
Tom Murphy
Phyllis Nagy
Anthony Neilson
Peter Nichols
Joe Orton
Joe Penhall
Luigi Pirandello
Stephen Poliakoff
Lucy Prebble
Peter Quilter
Mark Ravenhill
Philip Ridley
Willy Russell
Jean-Paul Sartre
Sam Shepard
Martin Sherman
Wole Soyinka
Simon Stephens
Peter Straughan
Kate Tempest
Theatre Workshop
Judy Upton
Timberlake Wertenbaker
Roy Williams
Snoo Wilson
Frances Ya-Chu Cowhig
Benjamin Zephaniah

For a complete listing of
Methuen Drama titles, visit:
www.bloomsbury.com/drama

Follow us on Twitter and keep up to date
with our news and publications
@MethuenDrama

Methuen Drama Modern Plays

include work by

Bola Agbaje
Edward Albee
Davey Anderson
Jean Anouilh
John Arden
Peter Barnes
Sebastian Barry
Alistair Beaton
Brendan Behan
Edward Bond
William Boyd
Bertolt Brecht
Howard Brenton
Amelia Bullmore
Anthony Burgess
Leo Butler
Jim Cartwright
Lolita Chakrabarti
Caryl Churchill
Lucinda Coxon
Curious Directive
Nick Darke
Shelagh Delaney
Ishy Din
Claire Dowie
David Edgar
David Eldridge
Dario Fo
Michael Frayn
John Godber
Paul Godfrey
James Graham
David Greig
John Guare
Mark Haddon
Peter Handke
David Harrower
Jonathan Harvey
Iain Heggie

Robert Holman
Caroline Horton
Terry Johnson
Sarah Kane
Barrie Keeffe
Doug Lucie
Anders Lustgarten
David Mamet
Patrick Marber
Martin McDonagh
Arthur Miller
D. C. Moore
Tom Murphy
Phyllis Nagy
Anthony Neilson
Peter Nichols
Joe Orton
Joe Penhall
Luigi Pirandello
Stephen Poliakoff
Lucy Prebble
Peter Quilter
Mark Ravenhill
Philip Ridley
Willy Russell
Jean-Paul Sartre
Sam Shepard
Martin Sherman
Wole Soyinka
Simon Stephens
Peter Straughan
Kate Tempest
Theatre Workshop
Judy Upton
Timberlake Wertenbaker
Roy Williams
Snoo Wilson
Frances Ya-Chu Cowhig
Benjamin Zephaniah

For a complete listing of
Methuen Drama titles, visit:
www.bloomsbury.com/drama

Follow us on Twitter and keep up to date
with our news and publications
@MethuenDrama

Printed in the USA
CPSIA information can be obtained
at www.ICGtesting.com
LVHW020944171024
794056LV00003B/948

9 781350 140523